50 Authentic Mexican Dishes You'll Crave

By: Kelly Johnson

Table of Contents

- Tacos al Pastor
- Enchiladas Verdes
- Chicken Mole Poblano
- Carnitas Tacos
- Chiles Rellenos
- Guacamole with Chips
- Tamales de Pollo
- Tacos de Asada
- Sopes de Carne
- Quesadillas with Mushrooms and Cheese
- Mexican Street Corn (Elote)
- Pozole Rojo
- Chilaquiles Rojos
- Tostadas de Atún
- Ceviche de Camarón
- Mole Negro with Chicken
- Burritos de Carnitas
- Fajitas de Pollo
- Flautas with Sour Cream
- Cochinita Pibil
- Sopa de Lima
- Churros with Chocolate Sauce
- Papas con Chorizo
- Queso Fundido
- Arroz con Pollo
- Elote en Vaso (Corn in a Cup)
- Albondigas (Mexican Meatballs)
- Tacos de Pescado
- Frijoles Charros
- Mexican Rice
- Tacos de Barbacoa
- Guajillo Chile Pork Carnitas
- Pollo en Adobo
- Tacos de Lengua
- Torta de Chorizo

- Poblano Cream Soup
- Sopes de Pollo
- Tamales de Rajas con Queso
- Mole en Salsa Roja
- Huaraches de Pollo
- Mexican Red Rice
- Enchiladas Suizas
- Chicharrón en Salsa Verde
- Caldo de Res
- Mexican Grilled Shrimp
- Tacos de Camarón
- Nopales con Queso
- Chile en Nogada
- Tacos de Papa
- Mole de Olla

Tacos al Pastor

Ingredients:

- 2 lbs pork shoulder, thinly sliced
- 1/2 cup pineapple, chopped
- 1 onion, chopped
- 2 cloves garlic, minced
- 2 tbsp achiote paste
- 1 tbsp chili powder
- 1 tsp cumin
- 1 tbsp apple cider vinegar
- Salt and pepper to taste
- 8 small corn tortillas
- Fresh cilantro, for garnish
- Lime wedges, for serving

Instructions:

1. In a blender, combine pineapple, garlic, achiote paste, chili powder, cumin, vinegar, salt, and pepper. Blend until smooth.
2. Marinate the pork slices in the mixture for at least 1 hour or overnight in the fridge.
3. Heat a large skillet over medium heat and cook the pork slices until browned and cooked through, about 8-10 minutes.
4. Warm tortillas and assemble tacos with the cooked pork, onion, and cilantro.
5. Serve with lime wedges on the side.

Enchiladas Verdes

Ingredients:

- 12 corn tortillas
- 2 cups shredded rotisserie chicken
- 2 cups green salsa (salsa verde)
- 1/2 cup sour cream
- 1/2 cup chopped onion
- 1 cup shredded cheese (cheddar or Mexican blend)
- Fresh cilantro, for garnish
- Salt to taste

Instructions:

1. Preheat the oven to 375°F (190°C).
2. Heat the tortillas in a dry skillet for about 30 seconds on each side.
3. Dip each tortilla in green salsa, then stuff with shredded chicken. Roll the tortillas tightly.
4. Place the rolled tortillas in a baking dish, seam side down.
5. Pour remaining green salsa over the top, then sprinkle with shredded cheese.
6. Bake for 20-25 minutes, or until the cheese is melted and bubbly.
7. Garnish with sour cream, onion, and cilantro before serving.

Chicken Mole Poblano

Ingredients:

- 4 chicken breasts
- 2 tbsp olive oil
- 1 onion, chopped
- 2 cloves garlic, minced
- 1/4 cup cocoa powder
- 1/4 cup peanut butter
- 1 tsp cinnamon
- 1 tbsp chili powder
- 1 tbsp cumin
- 2 cups chicken broth
- 1/2 cup tomato paste
- 1/4 cup brown sugar
- 1/4 cup sesame seeds
- Salt and pepper to taste

Instructions:

1. Heat olive oil in a large skillet over medium heat. Cook the chicken breasts until browned on both sides and cooked through. Remove and set aside.
2. In the same skillet, sauté onion and garlic until softened.
3. Add cocoa powder, peanut butter, cinnamon, chili powder, and cumin, and cook for 1-2 minutes.
4. Stir in chicken broth, tomato paste, brown sugar, and sesame seeds. Simmer for 10 minutes.
5. Pour the mole sauce over the chicken breasts and simmer for an additional 10 minutes.
6. Serve with rice and garnish with more sesame seeds.

Carnitas Tacos

Ingredients:

- 2 lbs pork shoulder, cut into chunks
- 1 onion, chopped
- 3 cloves garlic, minced
- 1 orange, juiced
- 1 lime, juiced
- 1 tbsp cumin
- 1 tbsp chili powder
- 1/2 tsp oregano
- Salt and pepper to taste
- 8 small corn tortillas
- Fresh cilantro, for garnish

Instructions:

1. In a large pot, combine pork, onion, garlic, orange juice, lime juice, cumin, chili powder, oregano, salt, and pepper.
2. Cover with water and simmer over low heat for 2-3 hours, until the pork is tender.
3. Shred the pork using two forks and return to the pot to soak up the flavors.
4. Warm tortillas and assemble tacos with the carnitas.
5. Garnish with cilantro and serve with lime wedges.

Chiles Rellenos

Ingredients:

- 4 poblano peppers
- 1 cup cheese (monterey jack or oaxacan)
- 1/2 cup flour
- 2 eggs, separated
- 1/2 cup breadcrumbs
- 1 cup tomato sauce
- 1 tsp cumin
- Salt to taste

Instructions:

1. Roast the poblano peppers on a grill or directly over a flame until the skins are blackened. Place in a bowl and cover with plastic wrap for 10 minutes.
2. Peel the skins off the peppers and remove the seeds. Stuff each pepper with cheese.
3. Beat egg whites until stiff peaks form. Mix the egg yolks with flour and salt.
4. Dip each stuffed pepper into the egg mixture, then coat in breadcrumbs.
5. Fry in hot oil until golden brown, about 3-4 minutes per side.
6. Serve with tomato sauce and garnish with cilantro.

Guacamole with Chips

Ingredients:

- 2 ripe avocados, mashed
- 1/4 cup red onion, finely chopped
- 1 jalapeño, minced
- 1/2 cup cilantro, chopped
- 1 lime, juiced
- Salt and pepper to taste
- Tortilla chips, for serving

Instructions:

1. In a bowl, mash the avocados until smooth.
2. Stir in onion, jalapeño, cilantro, and lime juice.
3. Season with salt and pepper to taste.
4. Serve with tortilla chips on the side.

Tamales de Pollo

Ingredients:

- 2 cups masa harina
- 1 1/2 cups chicken broth
- 1/2 cup vegetable oil
- 1 tsp baking powder
- 1 tsp salt
- 2 cups cooked chicken, shredded
- 1/2 cup green salsa (salsa verde)
- Corn husks, soaked

Instructions:

1. Mix masa harina, baking powder, salt, oil, and chicken broth until dough forms.
2. In a separate bowl, combine shredded chicken with salsa verde.
3. Take a soaked corn husk and spread a thin layer of masa dough in the center.
4. Add a spoonful of chicken mixture and fold the husk over to form a tamale.
5. Steam the tamales for 1-1.5 hours, until masa is cooked through.

Tacos de Asada

Ingredients:

- 2 lbs flank steak, marinated (with lime juice, garlic, cumin, and chili powder)
- 8 small corn tortillas
- 1/2 onion, chopped
- Fresh cilantro, for garnish
- Lime wedges, for serving

Instructions:

1. Grill the marinated flank steak to desired doneness, about 4-5 minutes per side.
2. Let the steak rest for a few minutes before slicing thinly against the grain.
3. Warm tortillas and assemble tacos with the steak, onion, and cilantro.
4. Serve with lime wedges.

Sopes de Carne

Ingredients:

- 1 lb ground beef
- 1/2 onion, chopped
- 1 tbsp cumin
- 1 tsp chili powder
- Salt and pepper to taste
- 8 sopes (thick corn tortillas)
- 1/2 cup refried beans
- Fresh lettuce, chopped
- Sour cream, for serving

Instructions:

1. Cook ground beef with onions, cumin, chili powder, salt, and pepper in a skillet until browned.
2. Heat the sopes in a dry skillet, then spread with refried beans.
3. Top each sope with the beef mixture, lettuce, and a dollop of sour cream.
4. Serve immediately.

Quesadillas with Mushrooms and Cheese

Ingredients:

- 4 large flour tortillas
- 2 cups mushrooms, sliced
- 1 cup shredded cheese (such as Oaxaca or mozzarella)
- 1 tbsp olive oil
- 1 small onion, sliced
- 2 cloves garlic, minced
- 1/2 tsp cumin
- Salt and pepper to taste
- Fresh cilantro, for garnish
- Sour cream, for serving

Instructions:

1. Heat olive oil in a skillet over medium heat. Add onions and garlic, sautéing until softened.
2. Add the mushrooms and cook until tender, about 5-7 minutes. Season with cumin, salt, and pepper.
3. Heat tortillas in a separate pan and sprinkle cheese evenly over one half of each tortilla.
4. Add the mushroom mixture on top of the cheese, then fold the tortilla in half.
5. Cook each quesadilla until golden and the cheese is melted, about 3-4 minutes per side.
6. Garnish with cilantro and serve with sour cream.

Mexican Street Corn (Elote)

Ingredients:

- 4 ears of corn, husked
- 1/4 cup mayonnaise
- 1/4 cup sour cream
- 1 tbsp lime juice
- 1 tsp chili powder
- 1/4 cup cotija cheese, crumbled
- Fresh cilantro, chopped
- Lime wedges, for serving

Instructions:

1. Grill the corn over medium heat until lightly charred, about 10 minutes.
2. In a small bowl, mix together mayonnaise, sour cream, lime juice, and chili powder.
3. Brush the grilled corn with the creamy mixture, coating evenly.
4. Sprinkle with cotija cheese and chopped cilantro.
5. Serve with lime wedges on the side.

Pozole Rojo

Ingredients:

- 2 lbs pork shoulder, cut into chunks
- 1 large onion, quartered
- 6 cloves garlic, smashed
- 2 dried ancho chilies
- 2 dried guajillo chilies
- 1 tsp cumin
- 1 tsp oregano
- 2 cups hominy (canned or frozen)
- 8 cups chicken broth
- Salt to taste
- Fresh cilantro, for garnish
- Sliced radishes, for garnish
- Lime wedges, for garnish

Instructions:

1. In a large pot, simmer pork shoulder, onion, and garlic in water for 2-3 hours until the meat is tender.
2. Toast the dried chilies in a dry pan for a few seconds until fragrant, then soak in warm water for 10 minutes.
3. Blend the chilies with a bit of the broth until smooth.
4. Add the hominy, chili mixture, cumin, oregano, and chicken broth to the pot. Stir well and simmer for 30 minutes.
5. Shred the pork and return it to the soup.
6. Serve garnished with cilantro, radishes, and lime wedges.

Chilaquiles Rojos

Ingredients:

- 12 corn tortillas, cut into strips
- 2 cups red enchilada sauce
- 1 cup shredded chicken (optional)
- 1/2 cup shredded cheese
- 1/4 cup sour cream
- 1/4 cup cilantro, chopped
- 1 small onion, sliced
- 2 eggs (optional)

Instructions:

1. Heat oil in a large skillet and fry tortilla strips until crispy. Drain excess oil on paper towels.
2. In the same skillet, pour the red enchilada sauce and bring to a simmer.
3. Add the fried tortillas, shredded chicken, and cheese. Stir to combine and cook until the cheese melts and tortillas are softened, about 5-7 minutes.
4. Optionally, fry eggs to serve on top.
5. Serve the chilaquiles topped with sour cream, cilantro, onion, and a fried egg if desired.

Tostadas de Atún

Ingredients:

- 2 cans of tuna, drained
- 1/4 cup mayonnaise
- 1 tbsp lime juice
- 1/2 cup diced cucumber
- 1/4 cup diced red onion
- 1/4 cup chopped cilantro
- 8 tostada shells
- Sliced avocado, for garnish
- Hot sauce, for serving

Instructions:

1. In a bowl, combine tuna, mayonnaise, lime juice, cucumber, onion, and cilantro.
2. Spoon the tuna mixture onto tostada shells.
3. Garnish with sliced avocado and drizzle with hot sauce.
4. Serve immediately.

Ceviche de Camarón

Ingredients:

- 1 lb shrimp, peeled and deveined
- 1/2 cup lime juice
- 1/2 cup lemon juice
- 1 medium tomato, diced
- 1 small red onion, diced
- 1/4 cup cilantro, chopped
- 1 cucumber, diced
- 1/2 avocado, diced
- Salt and pepper to taste
- Tortilla chips, for serving

Instructions:

1. Dice shrimp into small pieces and marinate in lime and lemon juice for 2-3 hours, until the shrimp is opaque and firm.
2. Mix the shrimp with tomato, onion, cilantro, cucumber, and avocado.
3. Season with salt and pepper.
4. Serve chilled with tortilla chips.

Mole Negro with Chicken

Ingredients:

- 4 chicken breasts
- 2 tbsp olive oil
- 1 onion, chopped
- 2 cloves garlic, minced
- 1/4 cup cocoa powder
- 1/4 cup peanut butter
- 1 tsp cinnamon
- 1 tbsp chili powder
- 2 cups chicken broth
- 1/4 cup tomato paste
- 1/4 cup brown sugar
- 1/4 cup sesame seeds
- Salt and pepper to taste

Instructions:

1. Heat olive oil in a large skillet over medium heat. Brown the chicken breasts on both sides, then remove and set aside.
2. In the same skillet, sauté onion and garlic until softened.
3. Add cocoa powder, peanut butter, cinnamon, chili powder, and chicken broth. Simmer for 10 minutes.
4. Stir in tomato paste, brown sugar, sesame seeds, salt, and pepper.
5. Return the chicken to the pan and simmer for another 15-20 minutes until the chicken is cooked through.
6. Serve with rice and garnish with additional sesame seeds.

Burritos de Carnitas

Ingredients:

- 2 lbs pork shoulder, cut into chunks
- 1 onion, quartered
- 3 cloves garlic, minced
- 1 orange, juiced
- 1 lime, juiced
- 1 tbsp cumin
- 1 tbsp chili powder
- Salt and pepper to taste
- 8 large flour tortillas
- 1 cup shredded lettuce
- 1/2 cup shredded cheese
- 1/2 cup sour cream
- Salsa, for serving

Instructions:

1. In a slow cooker, combine pork shoulder, onion, garlic, orange juice, lime juice, cumin, chili powder, salt, and pepper. Cook on low for 6-8 hours until the pork is tender.
2. Shred the pork with two forks and return it to the slow cooker to absorb the flavors.
3. Warm the tortillas and fill each with a generous portion of carnitas.
4. Top with shredded lettuce, cheese, sour cream, and salsa.
5. Roll up the burritos and serve.

Fajitas de Pollo

Ingredients:

- 4 chicken breasts, sliced into strips
- 1 bell pepper, sliced
- 1 onion, sliced
- 2 cloves garlic, minced
- 1 tbsp olive oil
- 1 tbsp lime juice
- 1 tbsp chili powder
- 1 tsp cumin
- 1/2 tsp paprika
- Salt and pepper to taste
- Flour tortillas, for serving
- Sour cream, guacamole, salsa, and lime wedges, for serving

Instructions:

1. In a bowl, combine chicken strips, lime juice, chili powder, cumin, paprika, salt, and pepper.
2. Heat olive oil in a skillet over medium-high heat. Add the chicken and cook until browned and cooked through, about 5-7 minutes.
3. Add the onion, bell pepper, and garlic to the skillet and cook for an additional 3-4 minutes until softened.
4. Serve the fajitas with tortillas and toppings such as sour cream, guacamole, salsa, and lime wedges.

Flautas with Sour Cream

Ingredients:

- 10 corn tortillas
- 2 cups shredded cooked chicken
- 1 cup shredded cheese
- 1/2 cup diced onions
- 1 tsp chili powder
- 1/2 tsp cumin
- Salt and pepper to taste
- Vegetable oil for frying
- Sour cream, for serving

Instructions:

1. Preheat the oil in a deep skillet over medium heat.
2. In a bowl, combine chicken, cheese, onion, chili powder, cumin, salt, and pepper.
3. Place a spoonful of the mixture onto each tortilla and roll them up tightly.
4. Fry the flautas in hot oil until golden and crispy, about 3-4 minutes per side.
5. Drain excess oil on paper towels and serve with sour cream.

Cochinita Pibil

Ingredients:

- 2 lbs pork shoulder, cut into chunks
- 1 onion, sliced
- 4 cloves garlic, minced
- 3 tbsp achiote paste
- 1/4 cup orange juice
- 1/4 cup lime juice
- 2 tbsp vinegar
- 1 tbsp cumin
- 1 tbsp oregano
- Salt and pepper to taste
- Banana leaves (optional, for wrapping)
- Small tortillas, for serving

Instructions:

1. Preheat the oven to 300°F (150°C).
2. In a blender, combine achiote paste, orange juice, lime juice, vinegar, garlic, cumin, oregano, salt, and pepper. Blend until smooth.
3. Place the pork in a large bowl and pour the marinade over the meat. Marinate for at least 2 hours or overnight in the fridge.
4. If using banana leaves, line a baking dish with the leaves.
5. Place the marinated pork into the dish, cover with the remaining leaves, and bake for 3-4 hours until the pork is tender and easily shred.
6. Shred the pork and serve with tortillas.

Sopa de Lima

Ingredients:

- 1 lb chicken breast
- 1 onion, chopped
- 2 cloves garlic, minced
- 1 bell pepper, chopped
- 4 cups chicken broth
- 2 limes, juiced
- 1 tsp cumin
- 1/2 tsp oregano
- 2 roma tomatoes, chopped
- 1/4 cup cilantro, chopped
- 2 corn tortillas, fried and cut into strips
- Salt and pepper to taste

Instructions:

1. In a large pot, cook the chicken breasts until fully cooked, then shred.
2. In the same pot, sauté the onion, garlic, and bell pepper until softened, about 5 minutes.
3. Add the chicken broth, tomatoes, cumin, oregano, and lime juice. Bring to a boil, then reduce heat and simmer for 15 minutes.
4. Add the shredded chicken and cilantro. Season with salt and pepper.
5. Serve the soup topped with fried tortilla strips.

Churros with Chocolate Sauce

Ingredients:

- 1 cup water
- 2 tbsp sugar
- 1/2 tsp salt
- 2 tbsp vegetable oil
- 1 cup all-purpose flour
- 2 eggs
- 1 tsp vanilla extract
- Cinnamon sugar, for coating
- 1/2 cup dark chocolate, chopped
- 1/4 cup heavy cream

Instructions:

1. In a saucepan, combine water, sugar, salt, and vegetable oil. Bring to a boil, then remove from heat.
2. Stir in the flour until a dough forms. Let cool slightly before mixing in the eggs and vanilla.
3. Heat oil in a deep pan over medium-high heat. Transfer the dough to a piping bag fitted with a star tip.
4. Pipe the dough into hot oil and fry until golden brown, about 3-4 minutes.
5. Drain on paper towels and coat in cinnamon sugar.
6. For the chocolate sauce, heat heavy cream in a saucepan and pour over chopped chocolate. Stir until smooth.
7. Serve churros with chocolate sauce.

Papas con Chorizo

Ingredients:

- 4 large potatoes, peeled and diced
- 1/2 lb chorizo sausage
- 1 small onion, chopped
- 2 cloves garlic, minced
- 1/2 cup cilantro, chopped
- Salt and pepper to taste

Instructions:

1. Boil the diced potatoes in salted water until tender, about 10 minutes. Drain and set aside.
2. In a skillet, cook the chorizo until browned. Remove excess fat.
3. Add the onion and garlic to the chorizo and sauté until softened.
4. Add the cooked potatoes to the skillet and fry until crispy.
5. Season with salt and pepper, and garnish with cilantro.

Queso Fundido

Ingredients:

- 1 lb Oaxaca cheese, shredded
- 1/2 cup chorizo, cooked and crumbled
- 1 small onion, chopped
- 2 tbsp olive oil
- Tortilla chips or tortillas, for serving

Instructions:

1. Heat olive oil in a skillet over medium heat. Add onion and cook until softened.
2. Add cooked chorizo and cook for another 2-3 minutes.
3. Lower the heat and add shredded Oaxaca cheese, stirring until melted and smooth.
4. Serve with tortilla chips or tortillas.

Arroz con Pollo

Ingredients:

- 2 chicken breasts, bone-in and skin-on
- 2 cups long-grain rice
- 1 onion, chopped
- 1 bell pepper, chopped
- 2 cloves garlic, minced
- 1 cup peas
- 2 cups chicken broth
- 1/4 cup tomato sauce
- 1 tsp paprika
- 1 tsp cumin
- Salt and pepper to taste

Instructions:

1. In a large pan, brown the chicken on both sides and set aside.
2. In the same pan, sauté the onion, garlic, and bell pepper until softened.
3. Add the rice and stir to coat.
4. Add chicken broth, tomato sauce, paprika, cumin, salt, and pepper. Bring to a boil.
5. Return the chicken to the pan, cover, and simmer for 20-25 minutes until the rice is cooked and chicken is tender.
6. Stir in peas and serve.

Elote en Vaso (Corn in a Cup)

Ingredients:

- 4 ears of corn, boiled or grilled and kernels removed
- 1/4 cup mayonnaise
- 1 tbsp chili powder
- 1/4 cup cotija cheese, crumbled
- 1 tbsp lime juice
- Salt to taste

Instructions:

1. Place the corn kernels in a cup.
2. In a small bowl, combine mayonnaise, chili powder, lime juice, and salt.
3. Spoon the mayonnaise mixture over the corn and top with cotija cheese.
4. Serve immediately with extra lime wedges.

Albondigas (Mexican Meatballs)

Ingredients:

- 1 lb ground beef
- 1/2 lb ground pork
- 1/4 cup rice, cooked
- 1/4 cup chopped cilantro
- 1 small onion, finely chopped
- 1 egg
- 1 tsp cumin
- 1 tsp garlic powder
- 1 tsp chili powder
- Salt and pepper to taste
- 2 cups tomato sauce
- 2 cups beef broth
- 2 cloves garlic, minced
- 1 small carrot, chopped
- 1 potato, peeled and chopped

Instructions:

1. In a large bowl, combine ground beef, ground pork, cooked rice, cilantro, onion, egg, cumin, garlic powder, chili powder, salt, and pepper.
2. Form the mixture into small meatballs, about 1 inch in diameter.
3. In a large pot, heat some oil over medium heat. Add the meatballs and cook until browned on all sides.
4. In the same pot, add minced garlic, carrots, and potatoes. Stir for a minute.
5. Add tomato sauce and beef broth, bring to a simmer. Cover and cook for 30-40 minutes, until meatballs are fully cooked and the vegetables are tender.
6. Serve the albondigas with the broth and vegetables.

Tacos de Pescado (Fish Tacos)

Ingredients:

- 1 lb white fish fillets (like tilapia or cod)
- 1 cup flour
- 1 tsp chili powder
- 1 tsp garlic powder
- 1/2 tsp cumin
- 1/2 tsp paprika
- Salt and pepper to taste
- Vegetable oil for frying
- Corn tortillas
- 1/2 cup shredded cabbage
- 1/4 cup cilantro, chopped
- 1 lime, cut into wedges
- Mexican crema or sour cream, for serving

Instructions:

1. In a shallow bowl, combine flour, chili powder, garlic powder, cumin, paprika, salt, and pepper.
2. Coat the fish fillets in the flour mixture.
3. Heat vegetable oil in a pan over medium heat and fry the fish until golden brown and crispy, about 4-5 minutes per side.
4. Warm the tortillas in a skillet or microwave.
5. Assemble the tacos by placing pieces of fried fish on each tortilla, and topping with shredded cabbage, cilantro, a squeeze of lime, and a drizzle of crema.
6. Serve immediately.

Frijoles Charros (Mexican Cowboy Beans)

Ingredients:

- 2 cups pinto beans, dried
- 1/2 lb bacon, chopped
- 1/2 lb chorizo, crumbled
- 1 onion, chopped
- 2 cloves garlic, minced
- 2 roma tomatoes, chopped
- 1 jalapeno, chopped
- 1/2 tsp cumin
- Salt and pepper to taste
- 4 cups water or broth
- Fresh cilantro, for garnish

Instructions:

1. Rinse and soak the pinto beans overnight or use the quick-soak method. Drain before cooking.
2. In a large pot, cook the bacon and chorizo over medium heat until crispy. Remove excess fat.
3. Add the onion and garlic and cook until softened.
4. Stir in the tomatoes, jalapeno, cumin, salt, and pepper. Cook for another 2 minutes.
5. Add the soaked beans and water or broth. Bring to a boil, then reduce to a simmer. Cover and cook for 1-2 hours, until the beans are tender.
6. Garnish with fresh cilantro and serve.

Mexican Rice

Ingredients:

- 2 cups long-grain rice
- 4 cups chicken broth
- 2 tbsp vegetable oil
- 1/2 onion, chopped
- 1 garlic clove, minced
- 1/2 cup tomato sauce
- 1/2 tsp cumin
- 1/4 tsp chili powder
- Salt to taste

Instructions:

1. Rinse the rice under cold water to remove excess starch.
2. Heat oil in a pot over medium heat. Add the rice and cook, stirring frequently, until lightly golden.
3. Add the chopped onion and garlic, cooking until softened.
4. Stir in the tomato sauce, cumin, chili powder, and salt.
5. Add the chicken broth, bring to a boil, then reduce the heat to low.
6. Cover and cook for 18-20 minutes, or until the rice is tender and the liquid is absorbed.
7. Fluff the rice with a fork before serving.

Tacos de Barbacoa (Beef Barbacoa Tacos)

Ingredients:

- 3 lbs beef chuck roast
- 3 cloves garlic, minced
- 2 tbsp apple cider vinegar
- 1 onion, chopped
- 2 tbsp chipotle peppers in adobo sauce
- 1 tbsp cumin
- 1 tbsp oregano
- 1/2 cup beef broth
- Salt and pepper to taste
- Corn tortillas
- Fresh cilantro, for garnish
- Lime wedges, for serving

Instructions:

1. In a slow cooker, combine the beef chuck roast, garlic, apple cider vinegar, onion, chipotle peppers, cumin, oregano, beef broth, salt, and pepper.
2. Cook on low for 6-8 hours, until the meat is tender and easily shreds.
3. Shred the beef with a fork and discard any fat.
4. Warm the tortillas and serve the barbacoa on each tortilla. Garnish with fresh cilantro and a squeeze of lime.

Guajillo Chile Pork Carnitas

Ingredients:

- 3 lbs pork shoulder, cut into chunks
- 4 guajillo chiles, seeds removed
- 2 cloves garlic
- 1 tsp cumin
- 1 tsp oregano
- 1/2 tsp cinnamon
- 1 tbsp lime juice
- 1 cup orange juice
- 1 onion, chopped
- 1 tbsp vegetable oil
- Salt and pepper to taste

Instructions:

1. In a blender, combine guajillo chiles, garlic, cumin, oregano, cinnamon, lime juice, and orange juice. Blend until smooth.
2. Season the pork with salt and pepper, then coat in the chile sauce.
3. Heat oil in a large pot over medium heat and sear the pork until browned on all sides.
4. Add the onion and cook until softened.
5. Cover and simmer for 2-3 hours, until the pork is tender and easily shreds.
6. Shred the pork with a fork and serve in tortillas.

Pollo en Adobo (Chicken in Adobo Sauce)

Ingredients:

- 4 chicken breasts
- 4 dried guajillo chiles
- 2 cloves garlic
- 1 tbsp apple cider vinegar
- 1 tbsp paprika
- 1/2 tsp cumin
- 1/4 cup olive oil
- Salt and pepper to taste

Instructions:

1. Toast the guajillo chiles in a dry pan over medium heat for a couple of minutes. Soak them in hot water for 15 minutes.
2. Blend the chiles with garlic, vinegar, paprika, cumin, olive oil, salt, and pepper until smooth.
3. Coat the chicken breasts with the adobo sauce and let marinate for at least 30 minutes.
4. Heat oil in a skillet over medium heat and cook the chicken for 5-6 minutes per side, until fully cooked.
5. Serve with rice or tortillas.

Tacos de Lengua (Beef Tongue Tacos)

Ingredients:

- 2 lbs beef tongue
- 1 onion, quartered
- 3 cloves garlic
- 2 bay leaves
- 1 tsp cumin
- 1/2 tsp oregano
- Salt and pepper to taste
- Corn tortillas
- Fresh cilantro and onions for garnish
- Lime wedges, for serving

Instructions:

1. In a large pot, cover the beef tongue with water and add the onion, garlic, bay leaves, cumin, oregano, salt, and pepper.
2. Bring to a boil, then reduce heat and simmer for 2-3 hours, until the tongue is tender.
3. Remove the tongue from the pot, peel off the skin, and shred the meat.
4. Warm the tortillas and serve the lengua with cilantro, onions, and lime.

Torta de Chorizo (Chorizo Sandwich)

Ingredients:

- 1/2 lb chorizo, casing removed
- 4 bolillo rolls or crusty rolls
- 1 avocado, sliced
- 1/2 onion, sliced
- Fresh cilantro, for garnish
- Salsa, for serving

Instructions:

1. Cook the chorizo in a skillet over medium heat until browned and fully cooked.
2. Split the bolillo rolls and toast them slightly.
3. Place a generous amount of chorizo in each roll.
4. Top with avocado slices, onion, cilantro, and salsa.
5. Serve immediately.

Poblano Cream Soup

Ingredients:

- 4 poblano peppers, roasted and peeled
- 1 medium onion, chopped
- 2 cloves garlic, minced
- 1 tbsp olive oil
- 4 cups chicken broth
- 1 cup heavy cream
- 1 tsp cumin
- Salt and pepper to taste
- Fresh cilantro for garnish

Instructions:

1. Roast the poblano peppers over an open flame or in the oven until charred. Place them in a bowl, cover with plastic wrap, and let them steam for 10 minutes. Peel and remove the seeds.
2. In a pot, heat olive oil over medium heat and sauté the onion and garlic until softened.
3. Add the roasted poblanos, cumin, and chicken broth. Bring to a simmer for 10 minutes.
4. Use an immersion blender to puree the soup until smooth, or transfer it to a blender.
5. Stir in the heavy cream and season with salt and pepper. Simmer for an additional 5 minutes.
6. Garnish with fresh cilantro and serve.

Sopes de Pollo (Chicken Sopes)

Ingredients:

- 1 lb chicken breast, cooked and shredded
- 12 small sopes (thick corn tortillas)
- 1/2 cup refried beans
- 1 cup lettuce, shredded
- 1/2 cup salsa roja
- 1/2 cup sour cream
- 1/2 cup crumbled queso fresco
- Fresh cilantro for garnish
- Salt and pepper to taste

Instructions:

1. Heat the sopes on a griddle or skillet until golden brown and slightly crispy.
2. Spread a thin layer of refried beans on each sope.
3. Top with shredded chicken, lettuce, salsa roja, sour cream, and crumbled queso fresco.
4. Garnish with fresh cilantro and serve.

Tamales de Rajas con Queso (Tamales with Poblano and Cheese)

Ingredients:

- 2 cups masa harina
- 1 cup chicken broth
- 1/2 cup vegetable oil
- 1 tsp baking powder
- 1/2 tsp salt
- 1/2 lb cheese, cut into strips (queso Oaxaca or mozzarella)
- 2 poblano peppers, roasted, peeled, and sliced
- Corn husks, soaked in warm water for 30 minutes

Instructions:

1. In a bowl, combine masa harina, chicken broth, vegetable oil, baking powder, and salt. Mix until the dough is smooth and has a dough-like consistency.
2. Spread a thin layer of masa on each soaked corn husk.
3. Add a few slices of poblano peppers and a strip of cheese in the center.
4. Fold the sides of the husk over the filling, then fold the bottom up to seal the tamale.
5. Steam the tamales in a large pot for 1-1.5 hours, until the masa is fully cooked.
6. Serve hot with salsa and crema.

Mole en Salsa Roja (Mole in Red Sauce)

Ingredients:

- 2 dried guajillo chiles
- 2 dried ancho chiles
- 2 tbsp sesame seeds
- 1 tbsp pumpkin seeds
- 1/4 cup almonds
- 1 tbsp cocoa powder
- 1/2 tsp cinnamon
- 1/4 tsp cloves
- 1 tbsp vegetable oil
- 1 small onion, chopped
- 2 cloves garlic, minced
- 2 cups chicken broth
- 1/2 cup tomato sauce
- Salt and pepper to taste

Instructions:

1. Toast the guajillo and ancho chiles in a dry pan until fragrant, then soak them in hot water for 15 minutes.
2. In a blender, combine the soaked chiles, sesame seeds, pumpkin seeds, almonds, cocoa powder, cinnamon, cloves, and a little bit of water. Blend into a smooth paste.
3. Heat the oil in a pot and sauté the onion and garlic until softened.
4. Stir in the mole paste, chicken broth, and tomato sauce.
5. Simmer for 15 minutes, stirring occasionally. Season with salt and pepper.
6. Serve the mole over chicken or your favorite protein.

Huaraches de Pollo (Chicken Huaraches)

Ingredients:

- 4 huarache-shaped tortillas (thick corn tortillas)
- 1 lb chicken breast, cooked and shredded
- 1/2 cup salsa verde
- 1/2 cup refried beans
- 1/4 cup crumbled queso fresco
- 1/4 cup sour cream
- Fresh cilantro for garnish
- Lime wedges for serving

Instructions:

1. Heat the huarache tortillas on a griddle until slightly crispy.
2. Spread a layer of refried beans on each tortilla.
3. Top with shredded chicken, salsa verde, queso fresco, and sour cream.
4. Garnish with fresh cilantro and serve with lime wedges.

Mexican Red Rice (Arroz Rojo)

Ingredients:

- 2 cups long-grain rice
- 4 cups chicken broth
- 2 medium tomatoes, blended into puree
- 1 onion, chopped
- 2 cloves garlic, minced
- 1/4 cup vegetable oil
- 1 tsp cumin
- 1/2 tsp chili powder
- Salt and pepper to taste

Instructions:

1. Rinse the rice under cold water.
2. Heat oil in a large pot over medium heat. Add the rice and cook, stirring occasionally, until golden brown.
3. Add the onion and garlic and cook until softened.
4. Stir in the tomato puree, cumin, chili powder, and salt.
5. Add the chicken broth and bring to a boil.
6. Reduce the heat to low, cover, and cook for 18-20 minutes, until the rice is tender and the liquid is absorbed.
7. Fluff the rice and serve.

Enchiladas Suizas

Ingredients:

- 12 corn tortillas
- 2 cups shredded chicken
- 2 cups salsa verde
- 1 cup heavy cream
- 1 cup shredded cheese (queso Oaxaca or Monterey Jack)
- 1/2 onion, chopped
- 1 tbsp vegetable oil
- Fresh cilantro for garnish

Instructions:

1. Heat the vegetable oil in a skillet over medium heat. Lightly fry the tortillas on both sides for 10-15 seconds, then drain on paper towels.
2. In a separate pan, heat the salsa verde and heavy cream together until warmed.
3. Fill each tortilla with shredded chicken and roll it up.
4. Place the rolled tortillas in a baking dish and pour the salsa verde mixture over them.
5. Top with shredded cheese and bake at 350°F for 20 minutes, or until the cheese is melted and bubbly.
6. Garnish with chopped onions and cilantro.

Chicharrón en Salsa Verde (Pork Skin in Green Sauce)

Ingredients:

- 1 lb chicharrón prensado (pressed pork skin)
- 2 cups salsa verde
- 1/2 onion, chopped
- 2 cloves garlic, minced
- 1/2 cup cilantro, chopped
- Salt to taste

Instructions:

1. Cut the chicharrón into bite-sized pieces.
2. In a large skillet, heat a little oil and sauté the onion and garlic until softened.
3. Add the chicharrón and cook until slightly crispy.
4. Stir in the salsa verde and cook for 10 minutes, letting the flavors combine.
5. Garnish with fresh cilantro and serve with tortillas.

Caldo de Res (Beef Soup)

Ingredients:

- 2 lbs beef shank with bone
- 4 carrots, peeled and chopped
- 2 corn on the cob, cut into pieces
- 3 medium potatoes, peeled and chopped
- 1 zucchini, chopped
- 1/2 small cabbage, chopped
- 2 cloves garlic, minced
- 1 onion, chopped
- 2 tomatoes, chopped
- 1 tsp oregano
- Salt and pepper to taste
- Fresh cilantro for garnish

Instructions:

1. In a large pot, combine the beef shank, garlic, onion, and enough water to cover. Bring to a boil, then reduce the heat to a simmer and cook for 1-2 hours, skimming off any foam.
2. Add the carrots, corn, potatoes, zucchini, cabbage, tomatoes, oregano, salt, and pepper. Simmer for an additional 30 minutes, until the vegetables are tender.
3. Garnish with fresh cilantro and serve.

Mexican Grilled Shrimp (Camarones a la Parrilla)

Ingredients:

- 1 lb large shrimp, peeled and deveined
- 3 tbsp olive oil
- 2 cloves garlic, minced
- 1 tbsp lime juice
- 1 tbsp fresh cilantro, chopped
- 1 tsp chili powder
- 1/2 tsp cumin
- Salt and pepper to taste

Instructions:

1. In a bowl, combine olive oil, garlic, lime juice, cilantro, chili powder, cumin, salt, and pepper.
2. Add the shrimp and toss to coat evenly. Let marinate for 15-30 minutes.
3. Preheat the grill to medium-high heat.
4. Thread the shrimp onto skewers and grill for 2-3 minutes per side, or until the shrimp are opaque and cooked through.
5. Serve with additional lime wedges and a side of your favorite salsa.

Tacos de Camarón (Shrimp Tacos)

Ingredients:

- 1 lb shrimp, peeled and deveined
- 1 tbsp olive oil
- 1 tsp chili powder
- 1/2 tsp cumin
- 1/2 tsp paprika
- 1/2 tsp garlic powder
- Salt and pepper to taste
- 8 small corn tortillas
- 1 cup shredded cabbage
- 1/4 cup cilantro, chopped
- 1 lime, cut into wedges
- Sour cream or crema for garnish
- Salsa of choice for garnish

Instructions:

1. Heat olive oil in a skillet over medium heat. Add shrimp and season with chili powder, cumin, paprika, garlic powder, salt, and pepper.
2. Cook the shrimp for 2-3 minutes per side, or until pink and opaque.
3. Warm the tortillas on a skillet or griddle.
4. To assemble the tacos, place a few shrimp on each tortilla. Top with shredded cabbage, cilantro, a squeeze of lime, and a dollop of sour cream or crema.
5. Serve with salsa on the side.

Nopales con Queso (Nopales with Cheese)

Ingredients:

- 4 fresh nopales (cactus pads), peeled and sliced
- 2 tbsp olive oil
- 1/2 cup onion, chopped
- 1 clove garlic, minced
- 1/2 cup crumbled queso fresco
- 1 tbsp fresh cilantro, chopped
- Salt and pepper to taste

Instructions:

1. Heat olive oil in a skillet over medium heat. Add the nopales and cook for 5-7 minutes, until they are soft and the sliminess has reduced.
2. Add the chopped onion and garlic and sauté until the onion is translucent.
3. Stir in the crumbled queso fresco and cilantro. Cook for another 2-3 minutes, allowing the cheese to melt slightly.
4. Season with salt and pepper to taste, then serve hot.

Chile en Nogada

Ingredients:

- 6 poblano peppers, roasted, peeled, and deseeded
- 1 lb ground pork or beef
- 1 medium onion, chopped
- 2 cloves garlic, minced
- 1/2 cup tomato, chopped
- 1/4 cup almonds, chopped
- 1/4 cup raisins
- 1/4 cup candied fruits, chopped (optional)
- 1 tsp cinnamon
- 1/2 tsp cloves
- Salt and pepper to taste
- 1/2 cup chopped parsley
- 1 cup walnut sauce (nogada)
- 1/2 cup pomegranate seeds for garnish

Instructions:

1. Heat olive oil in a pan over medium heat. Add the ground meat and cook until browned.
2. Add the onion, garlic, and tomato, and sauté until soft.
3. Stir in almonds, raisins, candied fruits (optional), cinnamon, cloves, salt, and pepper. Simmer for 5-7 minutes.
4. Stuff each roasted poblano pepper with the meat mixture and arrange on a plate.
5. Pour walnut sauce (nogada) over the stuffed peppers and garnish with parsley and pomegranate seeds.
6. Serve at room temperature.

Tacos de Papa (Potato Tacos)

Ingredients:

- 4 large potatoes, peeled and diced
- 1 tbsp olive oil
- 1/2 onion, chopped
- 1 clove garlic, minced
- 1/2 tsp cumin
- 1/2 tsp chili powder
- Salt and pepper to taste
- 8 small corn tortillas
- Fresh cilantro, chopped
- Salsa of choice

Instructions:

1. Boil the potatoes in salted water until tender, about 10 minutes. Drain and mash with a fork.
2. Heat olive oil in a skillet over medium heat and sauté the onion and garlic until softened.
3. Add the mashed potatoes, cumin, chili powder, salt, and pepper. Cook for another 5-7 minutes, stirring to combine the flavors.
4. Warm the tortillas in a skillet.
5. To assemble the tacos, spoon the potato mixture onto each tortilla.
6. Top with fresh cilantro and salsa.

Mole de Olla (Beef Soup with Mole)

Ingredients:

- 2 lbs beef shank with bone
- 1 medium onion, chopped
- 3 cloves garlic, minced
- 2 tomatoes, chopped
- 1/2 cup mole paste (you can use pre-made mole paste)
- 4 cups beef broth
- 2 carrots, chopped
- 2 potatoes, chopped
- 1 zucchini, chopped
- 1 cup corn kernels (fresh or frozen)
- Salt and pepper to taste
- Fresh cilantro for garnish

Instructions:

1. In a large pot, combine the beef shank, onion, garlic, and enough water to cover. Bring to a boil, then reduce the heat to a simmer and cook for 1-2 hours, skimming off any foam.
2. Add the chopped tomatoes and mole paste. Stir to combine.
3. Stir in the beef broth, carrots, potatoes, zucchini, and corn. Simmer for an additional 30 minutes, until the vegetables are tender and the flavors have melded.
4. Season with salt and pepper to taste.
5. Garnish with fresh cilantro and serve hot.

www.ingramcontent.com/pod-product-compliance
Lightning Source LLC
LaVergne TN
LVHW081330060526
838201LV00055B/2563